I0463561

Mega Projects Mega Realities

Harish Kumar

Published by Harish Kumar, 2020.

While every precaution has been taken in the preparation of this book, the publisher assumes no responsibility for errors or omissions, or for damages resulting from the use of the information contained herein.

MEGA PROJECTS MEGA REALITIES

First edition. April 2, 2020.

Copyright © 2020 Harish Kumar.

Written by Harish Kumar.

Why this Book

As International Inc continues to think big, business projects are getting bigger by the day. Search the maps of global business and look far and wide, you are sure to see mega projects mushrooming all over the place, as if there had been a torrential downpour of global ambitions.

Around the world, inspired project managers and their CEOs are rapidly realising that it is not just enough to dream big, they need to transform those dreams into mega projects and realities.

In fact, these inspired bunch of CEOs and project managers are mega devotees of size and scale today. Call them mega fetishists, if you prefer such a high-sounding word.

This penchant for gigantism in scale and size are furiously driving corporate plans and programmes, assets and ambitions forward today.

But, CEOs and project managers are also realising that size and scale mean new challenges. As projects turn Goliaths, smart management of mega projects is becoming critical for survival and success.

Flawless conception of projects and their efficient implementation, besides the ability to stick to pre-budgeted cost and time schedules, are becoming critical for survival and success in the dog-eat-dog global business world, both for the mega projects and project-implementing companies.

Naturally, project managers and their CEOs need to remember a few ground rules for managing mega projects with global competence. And face up to the challenging ground realities that are sure to develop *en route*.

What are these ground rules? What ground realities are waiting to confront them? What challenges are waiting to take them on?

Which mega project strategies are winsome? How Global Inc should be adopting these strategies and adapting to those of their competitors for better project management?

What should they do when they discover that chosen project technologies are not suitable for the available feedstocks and fail to fit into their budgetary frameworks and overall corporate schemes?

What should they do to prevent a time and cost over-run? Finally, how should they respond to changing federal regulations and laws?

Too many questions, and many more whirling in the heads of CEOs and project managers. They need convincing answers for all these questions in their quests for project excellence.

That is where this handy roadmap *Mega Projects Mega Realities* comes in. Whether you are a CEO or a project manager, you are sure to find this book extremely utilitarian.

Peppered with project anecdotes from India, *Mega Projects Mega Realities* has been written to offer project managers unforgettable lessons drawn from live-wire project instances and examples, project case studies and comments.

Well, do not wince on hearing mega project anecdotes are from India. Though mega project examples originate from Indian corporate heavyweights and consultancy majors, the lessons they provide here are certainly not region-specific. The project lessons here know no boundaries.

Anecdotes are dated, some might say. Sure, they have definite timelines. But, the lessons they throw are timeless, eternal, country-neutral and universal.

Remember, mega projects are the cement-and-steel representation of mega aspirations, mega dreams, mega desires and mega hopes.

Whether you are a mega project manager or an ambitious CEO or a maturing business school student, you are sure to find this mega projects manual illuminating.

Understand
Why manage Mega Projects

Managing mega industrial projects is a creative job and certainly not meant for the mechanical-minded. As markets go global, mega projects are becoming all the rage today.

Mega projects are the results of corporate ambition and are the final products of aspiration, assets and ability, and the insatiable desire to rule the world market.

When projects go mega, they send out a clear message that you have arrived.

Inflamed by such ambitions and aspirations, tempted by increasing access to global funds, and emboldened by their own prowess, corporate entities around the world are busy planning, designing, and executing industrial ventures on a size and a scale never heard or seen before.

With mega projects rising like tall towers even in controlled economies and in reserved-for-the-State sectors such as infrastructure, power-gas and telecom, the focus of mega projects is fast changing.

With that, the concept of size too is undergoing great changes. And scales are moving up almost across all industrial sectors and segments.

Of all the changes that the contagious liberalisation and privatisation continue to sweep in, diminishing role of state sectors and crumbling control-command economies are the most remarkable.

Gone are the days when projects were put up primarily to serve domestic markets. Today, projects are put up primarily to serve the *globalising* global markets.

That being the case, ambitious and projects-obsessed companies find themselves thrown to face domestic wolves, muscular MNCs and global Goliaths.

As economy after national economy integrates with the global economy, CEOs are rudely realising that their projects should be of minimum economic capacity by global standards, with minimum economies of scale.

Meanwhile, the very concept of what is minimum economic capacity has gone for a toss, changed for ever.

That is why mega projects are moving apace and gaining untold momentum. And managing them with mastery is fast becoming critical in all economies.

Add to this the rising need for investment-intensive public utility and infrastructure projects, it is not surprising that mega projects are banging impatiently on the doors of almost all the economies around the world.

Not surprising that the numbers of mega projects on paper and in progress are fast rising everywhere.

Disbursal statistics of World Bank and other global development banks present in the developing world clearly indicate that.

Expect such disbursals to mega infrastructure and development projects to move further up in the days to come.

Free and market-driven pricing of capital issues in most liberalised-liberalising economies and unhindered access to equity markets are certainly acting as catalysts.

The results are already evident: the sanctity around debt-equity ratios is vanishing.

Add to this the challenge thrown in by fast-crumbling tariff walls, business projects have to grow anything but bigger.

Earlier, institutional finance was integral to project finance. For, the depth of capital markets remained unplumbed. Such cramps are history now and buried well into the sunset region.

Thus, days of control were clearly marked by mega projects-unfriendly ecosystem. That is becoming history today and tomorrow promises to be a different day.

With free market-determined pricing of capital issues and the rising popularity of global depository receipts, the capacity to tie up finance has improved. That holds out much greater promise for mega projects.

Earlier, the sole route for financing the foreign exchange component of project cost was either through forex loans or export credits, largely underwritten by development finance institutions. At least that used to be the most accepted practice in developing economies.

Even that practice has been given the go-by now, thanks to the opening up of more avenues to raise the foreign exchange component of project cost. And that too without the irritants of bothersome guarantees.

Avenues such as international bond issues, global debt issues, global depository receipts, and Euro convertible issues, are open now for the dreamy project-promoters.

Thus, though finance continues to remain critical, even in a liberalised today, it is no longer a constraint.

In most mixed economies, industrial licensing was another major limiting factor. Imagine this factor was solely responsible for many promoters putting up projects, just because they had a licence for them. Forget the sector, forget the product and damn the world market! And who cares for the consumer? That was the thinking.

After many twists and turns, the story is different now. The sole consideration for putting up a mega project today is its profitability, its cash-generating capacity and its expected value-addition to investors.

All that is music to the ears of global investors. But, the music is jarring for the faint-hearted at home: mega projects need to be put up strictly within time and cost schedules. So that they are viable and profitable.

Thus, caveat number one here: project managers need to be more systematic and organised now in their approaches; and, stick to pre-drawn flowcharts.

Once project managers understood why moxie is must for managing mega projects, the mega battle is half won.

As projects get bigger by the hour, project managers are now needed to deliver on multifarious fronts.

These are: define project objectives, determine the components and constituent tasks involved, identify key project milestones, fix the length of each component task, allocate resources to each task, re-evaluate task relationships, schedule project tasks, pinpoint resource conflicts, and execute the project.

As projects turn mega, the job of the project manager too has gone mega now. It is now evident why you need to manage mega projects, and that too efficiently.

Clearly, mega projects management is more systematic and organised an approach that calls for the able backing of fine-tuned support monitoring systems.

All because the stakes involved are very high. So high that even minor lapses could lead to massive over-runs, cost-wise and time-wise, resulting in formidable financial losses, in the process jeopardising the very competitiveness of the mega project.

In the coming pages, this mini-handbook should take you through the most important mega project lessons you can ill-afford to forget.

All these lessons have been drawn from the rich and the varied experiences of celebrated project managers of blue-chip companies from the developing world.

Do not dismiss these lessons as dated. The mega project events here do have timelines, but the mega lessons they throw up are timeless. All lessons worth remembering for ever and forever.

Reality 1
Conceive Immaculately

No mega project idea is perfect in its entirety. Though it is difficult to conceive a mega project with cent per cent perfection, care and caution are needed in honing a mega project concept till its final blueprint is ready for approval. Here are a couple of practical and useful tips.

One, while conceiving a mega industrial project, take note of global capacities in the industry – present and potential. Know well who has how much capacity.

Two, consider global market conditions, the scenario in neighbouring markets, the trends in the markets of competing economies, global demand-supply configurations, international tariff barriers, emerging trends in global tariffs, and the expected duty levels in economies that matter.

In fact, factor in every global factor, with a bearing on your mega project's viability and operating efficiency. No wonder major players putting up mega projects often do a detailed SWOT analysis.

While conceiving a mega industrial project, it is very essential to work on the following assumption: in a couple of years, duty levels are going to move further down.

That means every mega project on the drawing board calls for mandatory factoring in of the global economics of the industry you are operating in. That is a must for an immaculate mega project conception.

Here is an interesting anecdote and it relates to the current *numero uno* among Indian corporates.

When the jewel in the Indian corporate crown Reliance Industries conceived its mega petrochemical project initially, the petrochemical industry was considered a sunrise sector. Thus, the mega project was projected to be profitable.

Alas, by the time the mega project was put up and commissioned, huge capacity build-ups elsewhere in the world, particularly in China and South Korea, made the project unviable.

How the mega petrochemical project was re-configured and turned around is another story.

That is why it is extremely crucial to conceive a mega project after factoring in the emerging global trends. Moreover, a mega project must remain globally cost-competitive and quality-competitive. Not just today, even tomorrow.

For the simple reason that the misplaced import-substitution argument that goaded promoters to put up mega projects, irrespective of their economies, stands discredited today. What is vital for the coming morrow is how effective the import-countering strategies are.

Willy-nilly, it has become a critical need today to re-work the arithmetic of a mega project: its cost, scale, size, funding structure and global viability and competitiveness. Even a minor lapse in any of these project calculations is sure to affect the cost-competitiveness of the mega project.

As global corporations operate in a compelling environment of competitive restructuring, it is also essential today that mega projects are conceived with possible mergers, potential acquisitions and scope for strategic alliances in mind.

Reality 2
Configure Finances Rightly

Finance is the lifeline of mega projects. As such, never forget the need for constant honing, regular fine-tuning and relentless monitoring of the mega project cost.

That should ensure the project cost remains reasonable and stays within limits; and the corporation's capital structure remains balanced. Naturally, corporations with mega projects today are opting for low debt-equity ratios and getting over their earlier obsession with expensive debt.

The rage to fund mega projects with economical equity is gradually spreading. With this equity cult catching up with investors, promoters are able to dream big and go for mega projects.

There are exceptions here, however. For instance, fertiliser projects need to be funded even today with huge debt. That is the case even today, even post-liberalisation in economies like India.

That is because administered pricing makes these ventures unattractive to equity investors.

In all other sectors such as petrochemicals, where free pricing of final products has been allowed, major chunks of project finance need to come through the equity route. And that is happening.

The fact that mega projects cannot afford to take credit risk for long is another reason why mega projects are resorting to higher equity.

Okay, debt is not going to be a bad word and, not banished for ever either. Debt does have its pride of place in the finance matrix of mega projects.

That is because the presence of debt helps to maximise investor-returns over the long haul, facilitating what corporate finance experts call "trading on equity" and offering equity-issuing corporations interest-driven tax-shelters.

That is why more result-oriented debt-equity structures are evolving worldwide. Do not overlook this trend.

Development finance institutions in developing countries increasingly prefer today a large equity component in a mega project's cost matrix.

But, individual saver-investors may like those mega projects with larger components of debt, with prospective returns in mind.

However, it is prudent for mega projects to strike the midpoint in the debt-equity curve. Whatever, finally that ratio should be determined on a case-to- case basis.

A 2:1 debt-equity ratio is generally acceptable, whatever be the industry. That means not just the right finance mix, even the right approach is needed in managing tricky mega project finances.

So, in pursuit of the right mega project finance mix, CEOs need to manage debt and equity effectively, all in the larger interests of the mega project, the corporation, their security-conscious creditors and their returns-obsessed equity investors. This often proves to be a tight rope walk. But, walk you must, without losing balance.

However, debt-equity mix is undergoing a change. Finance pros are willing today to scale up debt-equity even to 4:1, particularly in the case of capital-intensive utility projects.

Whatever, available evidence suggests they are now settling for larger equity today for mega projects. Indication: developmental finance institutions are stepping up assistance to such projects.

Consider: the power and steel projects of Shashi-Ravi Ruia-controlled Essar Steel (formerly Essar Gujarat) were first conceived with a moderate debt-equity ratio of 2:1 and 1:1 respectively.

The implication: if the prospects are promising, mega projects can opt for a higher proportion of risk capital and equity funds.

So, the loud and clear message is that corporations can raise higher equity capital today at a hefty premium, even for a greenfield project, which was not the case earlier. CEOs need to take note of such vital changes in the mega project finance matrix.

Another sticky area is the financing of the foreign exchange component of the mega project cost in developing economies.

The reality is that the cost of forex borrowings (inclusive of guarantee charges) is still within acceptable levels.

Naturally, it is still economical to borrow abroad than at home for ambitious corporations in fast developing economies.

Sure, such forex borrowings are generally resorted to meet the foreign exchange component of the mega project cost. However, there has been a noticeable rise in foreign exchange borrowings of mega projects-implementing corporations worldwide.

Even demand for deferred payment guarantees is moving up. CEOs cannot afford to ignore such signals.

Of late, many forex-borrowing mega corporations in developing economies have been wary of forex loans. That is because they fear that interest rates may firm up further and forex loans may become more expensive.

So, they are at best shying away from borrowing overseas and they are keen to borrow from assorted institutional lenders in their respective countries.

Expect this trend to gather momentum in the case of mega projects in most developing economies. One immediate fall-out of this trend is that promoters' contributions are moving up in mega projects.

By precedence and practice, these promoters are expected to fund as much as 20 per cent of the mega project cost. These days, this percentage can even go up to 30 per cent.

Meanwhile, rising cost of debt is heralding the advent of a lower debt-equity ratio of 2:1. Plus, mega projects today find a number of novel financing options opening up before them.

Cross-border leasing and offshore funding are some of them. It is high time CEOs and their financial controllers considered and explored these enticing options.

At the end of it, the bottom line is simple: financial risks of mega projects should be minimised at any cost. To do that, mega project promoters should tie up all necessary resources fully before beginning work on the project.

Remember, "all necessary resources" include not just financial resources, but all crucial clearances as well.

That is why mega project CEOs should ensure the in-principle and environmental clearances are in, well before the mega project takes off.

It is also necessary to make sure project finance support formalities such as underwriting contracts are signed and sealed before work begins on the mega project.

Consider this very illuminating instance from India Inc that proves this point.

Malvika Steel was a corporate entity promoted by one Vinay Rai. The company got into a major fix in the late Nineties. The reason: Rai failed to raise fully the funds needed for the project. That was primarily because Rai tried to meet the entire project cost through primary market offerings.

Again, another Indian corporate entity, Abhey Oswal-promoted Oswal Greentech (formerly Oswal Chemicals and Fertilizers and prior to that Bindal Agro Chem) found itself thrown on pins and needles in the late Nineties. Oswal and his mega project were never comfortable, right from the word go.

All because, like Rai, Abhey Oswal too plunged in with limited fund-raising capacity and credentials.

So, the million-tonne advice: have your entire mega project cost tied up well before taking the plunge into the project, well before even the first brick is placed on the project site.

Better still, make ample and adequate provisions for contingency funds to meet unforeseen developments.

Consider this real-life live-wire example that proves this point emphatically.

When the originally Aditya Birla-promoted mega project of Mangalore Refinery and Petrochemicals (now MRPL is a subsidiary and a division of the State-owned Oil and Natural Gas Corporation) was initially conceived in the late Nineties, a few heavyweight Birla officers and executives were keen on going ahead with the project even before the entire finance had been tie up and finalised.

For, they believed tying up the needed finance was just a matter of time. But, the late Aditya Birla saw to it that not even the land was purchased too early.

Reality 3
Plump for the Right Technology

Technology is one of the most critical inputs that determine the survival and success of mega projects. That is because a wrong choice could jeopardise the very viability of mega projects that may score high on many other counts.

Consider the case of Vikram Ispat, which was the original sponge iron division of Aditya Birla-controlled Grasim Industries. Currently, Vikram Ispat, known now as Welspun Maxsteel, is controlled by the Welspun Group.

The original mega sponge iron project of this Vikram Ispat makes an enlightening case study on the importance of right technology.

The project, conceived during the Nineties, opted for the untested and unproven Mexican HYL sponge iron technology and got into a mess.

Such a mess that the project cost moved up beyond control and considerably.

Needless to say that the technology choice was bad. Because, the Mexican HYL technology at best had a chequered global track record.

Here are the details of Vikram Ispat's ordeal. The ore for the project was sourced from the Hospet-Bellary mines and that ore had just minimum distribution of fine materials.

Though the USA-based Midrex has previous experience in putting up projects that use such ore, Birla, for some inexplicable reason, plumped for the unproven and untested Mexican HYL technology.

The consequence was terrible, resulting in much cash-burns and heartburns. What was the problem with the Mexican HYL technology?

Simple. Consider how the sponge iron process works to know and understand how simple the problem was.

Solid iron oxide was fed from the top of the reactor. Then it was reduced or de-oxygenated by the gas injected from below, thus resulting in direct reduced iron, DRI in abbreviated technical parlance.

Later, this DRI was hot-pressed into briquettes. In the case of Vikram Ispat's furnace, the feedstock material failed to flow smoothly downwards. The result was a *gooey* output.

Finally, the defect was discovered and it was at the discharge end of the reactor.

The defect was later rectified by removing the inserts. Thus, the passage was widened so that the desired output was obtained.

Fine. Why did Birla opt for the not-so popular and thus unproven and untested Mexican HYL technology? Here is the revealing support story.

L R Talwar, a Birla doyen of many a mega project, was just basking in the glory of his successful Birla mega project Indo Gulf Fertilisers.

Talwar was assigned the task of identifying the right technology for Vikram Ispat's sponge iron plant. He was fascinated by the Mexican HYL technology and so he toured extensively to study his favourite Mexican technology.

After witnessing the success of all those pilot plants using the Indian feedstock and employing the HYL technology, he returned and recommended that Vikram Ispat should opt for that Mexican HYL technology.

Talwar was also able to convince the Birlas that the HYL technology was competitive cost-wise too.

Alas! That was not to be. It proved to be a grave monumental error of judgment.

Why? All those plants based on Mexican HYL technology that Talwar saw were cold-discharging. So, Talwar had seen only the successful operation of cold-discharging pilot plants.

But, Vikram Ispat's plant was hot-briquetted and thus hot-discharging. And Midrex was the indisputable authority of hot-discharging plants. Birlas simply failed to realise then that it would be an expensive error.

What seemed to be a minor judgmental error ended up in making such an expensive difference, both in terms of time and money.

An additional outlay of over Rs 60 crore and an additional 15 months of project time, just to identify and rectify the defect.

Such costs resulting from wrong technology choices make project investments dead for a long period. And leads to unproductive expenses, which were close to Rs 400 crore in the case of Grasim's Vikram Ispat.

The message is loud, clear and stereophonic. Mega projects need to be carefully designed and commissioned.

Agreed, the much-harried Grasim's Vikram Ispat did sort out the problem later by switching to more expensive pellets as feedstock. But, that was again after a killing delay in advanced pelletisation and forward integration. Finally, Grasim learnt a lifetime lesson the hard way.

So, the mega message here for all the CEOs: do not settle even for the second-best technology. Only the best will do.

A few final words here. Sure, at times you may opt for the unproven technology, but only if that is really cost-competitive. And only after a thorough risk analysis.

Whatever, the Vikram Ispat anecdote clearly proves that choosing the right technology is not all that easy. It calls for due diligence, patience and perseverance.

Remember, there are too many technology suppliers all over the world, all tom-tomming their superiority. So, the best technology is difficult to buy, but it is not impossible.

The mega money question now is this: how do you go about evaluating diverse and different technologies?

Well, here is a simple, yet comprehensive, guide and solution: Do not shy away from comparing the different technologies available in terms of cost, feedstock availability, input suitability, degree of achievable product purity, energy efficiency, cost of production, and plant efficiency.

With the choice of the right technology, the mega project battle is nearly won.

Reality 4

Develop Project Management Skills

Begin the work on a mega project only after a careful selection of key project personnel. With so many mega projects going around, getting the right project people is going to be really difficult. Watch out, mega project leadership crunch is coming!

How excellent implementation, made possible by the carefully-selected team of key project personnel, can work wonders for a mega project is clearly demonstrated by Indo Gulf Fertilisers.

When the mega project was conceived, industrial licensing was still operational and free-pricing of capital issues was unheard of. Worse, the initial public offering bombed in the primary market.

But, that very same mega project is a winner today, thanks to cost-effective implementation, achieved through diligent application of perfect and consummate project management skills.

How did Indo Gulf Fertilisers move the mountains with the right project acumen and project management skills?

After the Bukhatirs of Bahrain failed miserably to muster the required resources for their 40 per cent stake, the Birlas quickly identified a top crack team of four the very day they decided to take up the 29 per cent refused by the otherwise mighty Bukhatirs.

So, the first message: lose no time in identifying the top project management team once the mega project is conceived and you are poised to take off. That means you are telling the world you are all set for the mega implementation.

After the team was in place, Birla and his crack team began exercising close control on the mega project. That was through regular reports, intense monitoring of project pace and brainstorming project sessions.

The result was concrete, it was there for all to see. The mega project was completed three months ahead of its budgeted time schedule.

Optimisation exercises pre-project too can help mega projects save on cost. Here is an anecdote, which drives home forcefully the point that there is no alternative to due diligence.

Humphreys & Glasgow was implementing a 1.2 million sponge iron project in India, based on Midrex technology, sometime during the Nineties.

During implementation, Humphreys had to reduce the quantity of structural steel to avoid cost over-runs.

After assessing all project inputs objectively, Humphreys altered the plant design suitably and trimmed the flab in the plant structure.

With the cost of structural steel high then, they were able to save a substantial per cent of the project cost.

Reality 5
Hone the Project Appraisal System

Earlier, project appraisals were run of the mill and they mostly pertained to the size aspect of the projects. Particularly in developing economies with control-command structures.

That was because risks were limited in protectionist and administered price regimes. But, today the risks are many and assorted, external and internal. That calls for a well-oiled appraisal mechanism, which has its rightful place in mega project management.

Earlier, if project management risks were taken care of, everything else was taken care of, almost auto. No longer, not today.

For instance, an entrepreneur putting up a refinery project today need to take into account the following factors and should have convincing answers to the following brain-wracking posers:

How long will the administered regime continue? Will the assured 12 per cent post-tax return be there for ever? What changes are possible in government policy towards pricing and imports?

Will import of liquefied petroleum gas and kerosene be allowed at lower duty rates? What infrastructural growth is expected in sectors such as transport that would have an impact on the movement of the final product?

And many more such brain-teasers, depending on the sector, the economy and the political dispensation.

These pre-project answers should be ready at hand today as financing institutions and appraising agencies are increasingly asking these questions. Even investors are.

Of late, appraisers have begun evaluating more critically the proposed time-schedule of mega project implementation and whether that time schedule is feasible.

They aren't stopping there. They are going ahead, along with the finicky financial institutions, monitoring the project progress chart closely.

They have a thumb-rule here: if the mega project is delayed by more than six months, it is alarming. For, the interest burden during that extended period could make the mega project unviable.

Another change in mega project appraisal is that appraising institutions are examining every mega project-category differently. Gone are the days when all projects were lumped together on an omnibus appraisal table.

So, honing your internal project appraisal system is fast becoming the need of the project hour. Consider this category-wise appraisal financial institutions are resorting to these days. Extra weightage is placed on the technology factor in the case of refinery projects.

Additional weightage is assigned to the potential market size factor in the case of steel and cement projects. Greater consideration is given to the emerging international scenario in the case of petrochemical projects.

The idea is to identify the most critical element of each mega project and then complete the appraising exercise.

There is here a pitfall in such subjective appraisal weightages. Thanks to their sheer size, mega projects can conceal deficiencies and thus such weightages can deceive.

Since mega projects increase lenders' exposures, lenders are setting up today project vigilance groups and honing prudential norms.

One such norm now institutional lenders follow in India is to downgrade the credit-worthiness of all the constituent companies in a business group, even if one of them defaults.

So, as a project promoter, ensure that all your companies are disciplined. The message: project homework is a must before the project proposal reaches appraisal agencies.

Reality 6
Build a Control Panoply

An effective project control process focuses on well-defined project tracking mechanisms, on measuring the results thrown up by such tracking mechanisms, and places considerable accent and emphasis on excellent team building and training.

Remember how project expert K W Abbott of the Texas-based Stone & Webster Inc outlines five critical steps of an effective project control process.

These steps, equally and eminently, apply to all mega projects. Here they are, as a recap, in capsules:

* Identify and understand the process, break it down into manageable-size work packages, and standardise each package.

* Establish a construction-driven approach to project execution that ensures engineering and procurement support.

* Develop and adopt standard project control tools that best measure work process performance.

* Train project teams to understand the means by which projects are completed.

* Empower lead engineers on projects to act as frontline process problem-solvers.

What is essential for the success and survival of a mega project is this: A well-honed and fine-tuned project management system that ensures control over mega project scheduling and costing, and that facilitates smooth and seamless co-ordination among all project-participants. This is an absolute.

Thus, one finds greater application of critical path method models and project organisation charts today. And greater care is now being exercised in the recruitment of middle-level project personnel.

Project managers need to have a quality man today as a part of the mega project organisation. His responsibility will be to oversee and monitor the quality of every mega project input.

Another must-input for project control is an effective vendor surveillance system for ensuring compliances. Such a system of vendor surveillance is essential for all mega projects, primarily for avoiding slippages in various engineering designs, in fabrication of equipment and in their supplies.

Since legislative requirements such as adherence to pollution control norms, industrial emission standards, industrial safety guidelines, and effluent treatment standards have to be complied with, the need for vendor surveillance has become all the more critical for mega projects.

Remember speedy clearances are bound to become easier once such vendor surveillance system is put in place.

Project monitoring is another area where project control systems are needed and should be put in place so that regular monitoring of cost and time schedules are done.

As global economy and industry are in a flux, do not ignore the need for monitoring the time and the cost schedules of mega projects regularly. Such monitoring is integral to project control systems today.

Ignore such ongoing monitoring and your own project's survival is damned.

This canon equally applies to the monitoring of cost-schedules. It is high time you realised a project budget gone haywire can put the entire business of the corporate entity in question out of kilter.

Corporations with quite a few mega projects in progress need to keep comparing their progress so that controls can be built in those projects that are lagging behind.

Building such strong and formidable project control panoply should go a long way in making mega projects win-win propositions outright.

Reality 7
Remember to Manage the Contractor

It is a well-known fact that appraisers favour mega projects that are entrusted to a turnkey contractor. That is why, of late, institutional appraisers are looking at whether the implementation of a mega project has been awarded to a turnkey contractor.

The rationale: even if it means shelling out more, it is safer for a corporation to shell out a little more and get its project commissioned on time, with all implementation risks passed on to the turnkey contractor.

The key thus lies in the choice of the right turnkey contractor. The global trend is to opt for the co-operative consortium implementation. For, consortium means project resources are pooled and project risks are shared.

Remember to choose a turnkey contractor who is on your wavelength. That is critical. Since a mega project is teamwork, working with the client and thinking like him is essential. So, the need is for effective alliancing between the main contractor and all the sub-contractors.

Such a well-knit relationship helps every contractor to know what the other wants. Thus, achieving smooth co-ordination among project participants and avoiding duplication of efforts become easier.

Essentially, efficient contractor management involves setting definite project targets right from the word go. That should make project participants fully aware of what is expected from them.

And enable every one to operate in full knowledge of project objectives and budgeted returns.

It has been proved time and again that effective alliancing helps to align mega project objectives and achieve superior results.

All the above premises and arguments clearly establish that efficient mega project management calls for choosing the right contractor, preferably turnkey, tactful handling of that chosen contractor, and above all productively interacting with him.

Towards this goal, it is essential that the mega project-promoter does the following, diligently:

* Let the contractor understand the corporate organisation through effective and continuous communication.

* Grant formal approval on time to all mega project documents – contract agreement, project co-ordination procedures, process design, basic engineering specifications, site plans, plot plans, mechanical flow-sheets, electrical line diagrams and project schedules.

* Not to approve project documents until they are completed, reviewed and checked internally.

* If mega project documents are not approved, state the reasons why they are not, so that the contractor can revise and resubmit them for fresh approval.

* As far as possible, make no further changes once the documents are formally approved.

* Ensure there is no conflict between your contractor's approach and your approach towards all your projects. Let all projects work in tandem towards the common corporate goal. Ensure the contractor is aware of your project objectives and the overall goals of your organisation.

The Last Word

The central message in all these realities and lessons cannot be missed. Win-win mega project management transcends the demands of maximising returns or the belligerent thrusts of global corporations rampaging into developing economies.

To be sure, prospering according to the parameters of accomplishment is no mean task. But, at another level, this success embraces the fundamental concept of managing amidst mega chaos.

That is because mega project management is all about total control – all through conception and delivery – in an environment, where perpetual change is the only constant. Such a total control is needed for ever, even long after the mega project has gone on stream.

Simply, you cannot afford to fail. Fail, and you would have fallen victim to the ruthless forces of Darwinian competition that spares none but the fittest.

Succeed, and you would have proved your ability to impose a mega method amidst the madness of global markets.

Also by Harish Kumar

Metaphoric Madness
Metaphoric Madness
More Metaphoric Madness
Much More Metaphoric Madness
Not The End of Metaphoric Madness

Standalone
Mega Projects Mega Realities
Canons of Corporate Surgery
Conspiracies of Colours
Politics of Eponyms
Who Took the Orange from my Rainbow?
Winking in Wunderland
The Post-Pandemic Planet